Original title:
Hats and Horizons

Copyright © 2025 Creative Arts Management OÜ
All rights reserved.

Author: Aurora Sinclair
ISBN HARDBACK: 978-1-80586-096-9
ISBN PAPERBACK: 978-1-80586-568-1

Shelter from the Sun

A floppy cap atop my head,
It flaps like wings, and I feel fed.
With shades so dark, I strike a pose,
I'm cooler than a garden hose.

A squirrel once stopped, took a good look,
Thought I was food or maybe a book.
I waved goodbye as it did flee,
Just a sunshade, not a tree!

A Threaded Escape

My beanie's on, it fits just right,
It guards my thoughts, both day and night.
A classic curl, a style to keep,
It whispers secrets while I sleep.

A pom-pom pops, a bouncing cheer,
A tiny friend that's always near.
When friends all laugh at my headpiece,
I jester well — it's a great increase!

Beyond the Crest

A straw lid, my favorite attire,
It shields my dreams, ignites the fire.
In winds that dance, it takes a flight,
My trusty partner, pure delight.

With each new step, it twirls and sways,
Through grassy fields, the sunlight plays.
A fusion of giggles and sun rays,
Makes for endless funny days!

Woven Wanderlust

A knitted cap adorned with flair,
I saunter forth without a care.
It bobbles high, a carnival sight,
Makes every walk feel just so bright.

A dance party in my woolly dome,
Torres of joy, I roam and roam.
With every twist and turn I make,
A giggle pops — for goodness' sake!

The Summit of Style

On top of my head, a cloud does sit,
A grand old cap, just a little too fit.
It's dancing with wind, what a sight to see,
A fashion statement, just for me!

Each feather a story, each patch a laugh,
It's crooked and silly, like a math class gaffe.
The squirrels are jealous, the birds look bemused,
At this summit of style, I'm both blessed and confused.

Chasing the Canopy

I wore a sombrero, bright as the sun,
Chasing the branches, oh what fun!
Trees wearing crowns, the leaves in delight,
Their laughter echoed, a silly sight.

An umbrella's twirl, in a gusty breeze,
Became my companion, as I skated with ease.
We danced through the park, in a wonderful show,
A carnival of colors, wherever we'd go.

Adorning Aspirations

My dreams wear a bowler, quite out of place,
With visions so wacky, they're quite a showcase.
A top hat of hopes, tumbling down,
With every wild whim, I embrace the clown.

A beanie of wishes, so cozy and warm,
It keeps my ambitions safe from all harm.
I tip them to passerby, with flair and flair,
Spreading giggles and joy everywhere!.

Threads to the Beyond

My yarn is a portal, of colors galore,
A tapestry spinning, with laughter in store.
Each stitch a memory, here and afar,
My knitted creations, now reach for the stars!

With a scarf made of giggles, a cap of delight,
I thread through this world, oh what a sight!
Winding and looping, on this journey I find,
That laughter and style are perfectly entwined.

Ornaments of the Open Air

A cat in a beret, quite the sight,
Prowling the rooftops, full of delight.
Seagulls wearing shades, so cool and spry,
Chasing the sun, oh me, oh my!

Kites dance like dancers, flying so high,
With bows and ribbons that flutter and fly.
A squirrel in a cap, at the tree's top,
Waving to pigeons, who won't ever stop.

Tethered to the Wind

A fellow with a feather, what a show,
Twisting and turning like he's in a flow.
A breeze sends him spinning, round and round,
While the trees just laugh at the silliness found.

Up, up, and away, what's that in the sky?
A fish in a trench coat, how to apply?
He bounces on clouds with a grin so wide,
While clouds puff and chuckle, they just can't hide.

Helmets of Hope

A brigade of bumblebees in hard hats,
Buzzing along like the silliest of brats.
Twirling around flowers like they're in a race,
With a bumble of laughter painted on each face.

A snail in a helmet, oh what a sight,
Crawling so slow, yet feeling just right.
With optimism flowing, it shines through the shell,
Laughing at time, he knows it too well.

Roofs of Reflection

A frog on a rooftop, croaking a tune,
With shades on his eyes, oh, he thinks he's a boon.
The sun is a mirror, the sky is a grin,
As he jumps from the top, lithe as the wind.

In a top hat, a sheep, doing a quick jig,
Dancing with rabbits, all seen from the gig.
While the moon winks softly, rolling with glee,
The night wraps them up in a tapestry.

The Uncharted Canopy

In a world where headwear grows,
Fluffy puffs and jellybeans,
Top hats dance in twirling rows,
Bouncing on bouncy trampoline scenes.

A cap with wings took off one day,
Soaring high in the bubbly air,
Dodging clouds in laughter's play,
While others giggled without a care.

Fedoras tipped, the sun went bright,
Nose tickled by the breeze's blow,
Laughing gnomes in feathered flight,
Spinning tales of friends we know.

Oh, what fun this merry chase!
Each dome a story, bold and wild,
Chasing cheer across wide space,
In this whimsical world, we're all a child.

Topping the Unseen

A bowler rolls atop a hill,
Jolly poppies peek and smile,
Yet sneaky squirrels plot their thrill,
To steal those toppers for a while.

Caps that giggle, wigs that sing,
Each tip a twist of wacky glee,
Balmy breezes make them swing,
Hopping jigs for all to see.

From straw to silk, they flip and flop,
As careless birds take note with pride,
Every jump a joyful plop,
In the game of hats, we confide.

Why do they dance? We do not know,
Just chuckles loud, no hint of frown,
In their playful hats, they steal the show,
Wearing whimsy like a crown.

Wings of a Dreamer

A cap with dreams took flight at dawn,
Gliding past the giggling trees,
Whirling thoughts felt light as pawns,
Riding high on playful breeze.

With cheeky brims and ribbons tight,
They whisper secrets to the stars,
Plotting mischief in moonlit night,
Before dawn arrives with silly cars.

Feathered friends with zany flair,
Wadded hats that spin around,
Crafting laughter high in air,
While gravity forgets its ground.

So come and join this quirky race,
Where chapeaus waltz like they're alive,
Each twirl's an act of pure embrace,
In a saga where the fun will thrive.

Velvet Vistas

Upon my head, a quirky thing,
A rabbit's tail, a feathered wing.
It flops and bounces with each step,
Like me, it loves to laugh and prep.

The neighbors stare as I parade,
In colors strong, a bold charade.
They point and chuckle, what a sight,
My velvet crown brings pure delight.

Waves of fabric, oh so grand,
In a dance, we take a stand.
Each twist and twirl, a playful cheer,
With joy and whimsy, all draws near.

So if you're down and feeling blue,
Just find a hat and join the crew.
Slip on a smile, let laughter fly,
In this parade, we all comply.

Daydreams in Wool and Woolens

Knitted dreams atop my crown,
A llama pranced, he wouldn't frown.
Each stitch a giggle, bright and bold,
A woolen story waiting to be told.

It fluffs and puffs, creating cheer,
A fuzzy cloud that's drawing near.
With every bobble that I sport,
I'm king of laughter, my own court.

The evening breeze, a playful tease,
A tickle from the ends of fleece.
I tip my cap to passersby,
And wink beneath the twilight sky.

So join the fun, don't stay aloof,
Let's knit our dreams, let laughter proof.
In colors bright, we roam the night,
With every giggle, pure delight.

Crowning Dreams

Upon my head, a towering feast,
Of chocolate hats, a sugary beast.
With sprinkles bright, oh what a sight,
Each bite of laughter feels just right.

A party scene atop my dome,
A cat and dog, they feel at home.
They dance around, my loyal mates,
In wacky hats, they rule our fates.

With jellybeans and licorice strings,
We sway and twirl, oh how it swings.
Our antics bold, our giggles loud,
A wacky bunch, we stand so proud.

So take your bow, wear something grand,
Let's pack the town, just like we planned.
In this mad hatters' grand parade,
With every laugh, our worries fade.

Veils of Distant Skies

A curtain fluttering, oh what a tease,
With stars that wink among the trees.
My top hat spins with every whirl,
While moonbeams tickle and gently twirl.

In veils of color, dreams collide,
A jester's charm, a lucky stride.
We frolic through the fields of lore,
Where laughter fills the air once more.

The breeze hums tunes of playful glee,
As kites and hats dance wild and free.
With every gust, new friends appear,
In this tapestry of fun and cheer.

So don your finest, come what may,
Let's march together, bright and gay.
In skies so vast, we'll share our glow,
With laughter ringing from head to toe.

Adorned Journeys

On my head, a quirky lid,
It floats like dreams, oh what a kid!
With feathers bright and colors loud,
I strut around, feeling proud.

A floppy cap that flops and sways,
Chasing pigeons on sunny days.
I trip and laugh, don't take a fall,
My silly crown? I flaunt it all!

The sun peeks in, with cheeky grins,
I juggle snacks and make my spins.
With every step, adventures start,
Each silly hat, a work of art.

Oh what a ride, this wacky spree,
As laughter dances, wild and free.
These travels bright, they never tire,
In my jovial gear, I shoot for higher!

A Sky Full of Dreams

I wear a cap that's shaped like cheese,
Under clouds that giggle and tease.
With dreams swirling, a wobbly sight,
I float through days with pure delight.

A rainbow scarf wrapped 'round my chin,
The world's a stage, let the fun begin!
Each silly thought, a kite in flight,
Carried by whim, day turns to night.

I tap dance on the edges of fun,
With popcorn caps, I'm never done.
The sun winks down, my hat a crown,
As I twirl about, no chance of frown.

With every giggle, the sky expands,
A universe built by happy hands.
So grab a laugh, let worries slip,
For in this hat, I sail and rip!

Outfitted for Discovery

With goggles perched atop my dome,
I search the world, my silly home.
A bit of flair, an old straw hat,
I venture forth, grand as a cat.

My coat is polka dots, so tight,
I bump into smiles, and that's alright.
With a map that leads to candy doors,
Every step, I explore some more!

Oh look, a bird with a silly grin,
It calls me forth, let the fun begin!
In my mismatched shoes, I dance the way,
Across the trail where laughter plays.

Each treasure found, a quirky beast,
With every laugh, I become the feast.
No need for plans, just spread the cheer,
Outfitted for joy, I hold it dear!

Crowns Against the Sky

A crown of blooms atop my head,
Painted skies and pinky-red.
Each flower sings a silly tune,
As I sway and dance 'neath the moon.

A jaunty hat with bells that jingle,
As I hop and skip, oh how I mingle!
With clouds of fluff as friends nearby,
We laugh and leap, oh my, oh my!

The sun is bright, it pokes and prods,
While wacky styles get all the nods.
In every giggle, memories blend,
Each hat a chapter, never to end.

So here's to crowns both wild and spry,
Adorning dreams that touch the sky.
With each new glance, we giggle and sigh,
In our wonderful world, we always fly!

Crowning the Journey

On my head, a wild green cap,
It bounces with every step I tap.
Birds laugh and join the show,
As I strut like I'm in a row.

A floppy hat, with flowers bright,
Makes me feel like a dazzling sight.
I wave to the clouds, they wave right back,
A hat parade on this silly track.

As sunbeams dance upon my crown,
I twirl around, then tumble down.
With each cap tweak, giggles ensue,
A funny fest, just me and you.

In every shape and size they fit,
My wobbly style is quite the hit.
With feathers here and sequins there,
Let's tip our heads and lighten the air!

Distant Vistas

I spy a skyline up ahead,
Wearing sunglasses, the city's fed.
Its silly grin, a skyline joke,
While clouds above start to poke.

The mountain's wearing a beanie tight,
In a snowstorm, oh what a sight!
With a wink it starts to sway,
A jovial giant in white ballet.

Beneath it all, a cacti hat,
Wobbly hatpins that go splat!
Nature's laughter fills the void,
While I strut round, all overjoyed.

Each view's a giggle, a playful tease,
As horizons spill like melted cheese.
With each glance far, a chuckle grows,
For distant sights with funny clothes!

Threads of Exploration

I'm off to the world, with threads galore,
A patchwork cap, what's behind door four?
Each fabric tells a different tale,
Of adventures grand, where dreams set sail.

A polka dot swipe, a stripe parade,
With every twist, a joke is made.
Lace and linen, winks and flares,
A tapestry of goodness, none compares.

Fabrics flap in the wind so bold,
Stories of wonder, yet untold.
With every knot, a laugh we find,
In threads that tickle, oh so kind.

From city to meadow, I hear them sing,
My hat and I, we're the jester's king!
On this quilted quest, we prance and cheer,
With every step, the fun draws near.

The Veil of Adventure

A veil floats gently, soft and light,
Whirling with laughter, what a delight!
It wraps around with whispers sweet,
As I dance to a whimsical beat.

Each corner turns, a chuckle found,
As faces peek from underground.
My veil is full of stories bright,
With silly twists that take to flight.

Beneath it all, a comical twist,
Ideas pop like bubbles, can't resist!
The wind plays tag, pushing me fast,
While giggles trail in a silly blast.

With every flutter, the jokes ignite,
Casting shadows of pure delight.
So here's to the fun, let's lift the shade,
In the veil of joy, adventures are made!

The Boundless Peak

Atop the world, a cap so grand,
It caught the breeze, a playful hand.
A squirrel stopped to give a stare,
And wondered what was up with flair.

The mountain grinned with snowy face,
As beanies danced in woolly grace.
A parrot squawked, 'You look quite bold!'
While climbers sang of tales retold.

Beyond the Fabric

A shimmery scarf caught the light,
It twirled and twisted, oh what a sight!
A rabbit hopped right into the flow,
Dressed like a dandy for the show.

With each new wave, a pattern formed,
The laughter of weavers, hearts warmed.
A dog in a vest, with shades on tight,
Declared, 'This party's out of sight!'

Decorated Destinations

A bus stop gleamed with caps and crowns,
Where drivers honked and wore their gowns.
A bear in bowler waved hello,
To tourists lost in cheery woe.

With every train that rolled on by,
A top hat soared, oh me, oh my!
And folks would cheer as feathers flew,
While pigeons strutted, 'How do you do?'

Stitched with Aspiration

In a tailor shop, all colors gleamed,
The threads of laughter, they all dreamed.
A button flew as tales were spun,
Of fashions past and silly fun.

A spool of thread danced on the floor,
Sewing mischief by the score.
With each new stitch, life's punchlines grew,
And echoed joy, as if they knew!

High Altitude Dreams

In a world where high tops roam,
Clouds wear caps that feel like home.
With every breeze, the laughter swells,
Each fluffy lump a story tells.

Dare to climb the peak so tall,
With a goofy grin, just risk the fall.
The sun's a jester in the sky,
While all the mountains wear a tie.

Witty winds with playful furls,
Swirl around the goofy swirls.
Chasing shadows of silly sights,
As giggles dance on paper kites.

So lift your spirits, let them soar,
In this capered space, there's always more.
Where heights bring giggles and dreams afloat,
On ridiculous clouds, we find our boat.

Capping the Day

At the peak of twilight's call,
We tip our caps and jest a brawl.
With twilight shadows, we combine,
To set the mood for silly times.

A quirky cap adorned with flair,
Twirls upon the noggin, fair!
As stars begin to shine and twinkle,
Our laughter dances with each sprinkle.

With cozy wraps and playful grins,
Embracing fun where the day begins.
The sun scoffs as it fades away,
We sip on joy, come join the play!

So let's cap off this day so bright,
With silly joys that last through night.
In every chuckle, let's make a toast,
To the little things we cherish most!

Follicles of Fortitude

With each strand dancing on my head,
Resilience grows, no room for dread.
Each curl a story, twists and turns,
Filled with laughter, wisdom burns.

Bold wigs and hats, a playful troop,
In this arena, wigs do swoop.
Frizzy moments, styling frolics,
Life's mishaps turn to comical antics.

The world's a stage for our grand display,
Where styles clash and humor plays.
From fuzzy buns to wild sprays,
Courage shines in these merry ways.

We sport our looks with happy glee,
Eccentric silhouettes, can't you see?
In this hair-raising joy parade,
Fortitude blooms, and fears do fade.

Curved Visions

With lenses round, the world appears,
In frames of laughter, no room for tears.
Curved and bright, the colours spin,
In playful worlds, we leap right in.

Gazing afar with giddy cheer,
Every outlook brings us near.
Wacky shapes and styles galore,
Making bears wear silly decor.

Spectacles take the lead this day,
Turning frowns to giggles, come what may.
As visions swirl like candy canes,
Life's full of fun, and joy remains.

So grab your frames and join the show,
In silly sight, we freely flow.
Where every glance opens the door,
To wit and charm, forever more!

Nature's Canopy

Under leaves that sway and dance,
A squirrel dons a thrift shop pants.
Birds gossip in their feathery best,
While ants host a tiny fashion fest.

Sunbeams peek through branches wide,
A raccoon wears a top hat with pride.
Grasshoppers leap in a jubilant cheer,
While butterflies twirl with no hint of fear.

Beneath the sky, a giggle escapes,
As frogs race around in cloaks and capes.
Squirrels compete for the finest attire,
Each stitch a spark of woodland fire.

Nature's runway, a sight to behold,
With outfits made of green and gold.
The critters strut with a whimsical grace,
In this merry, vibrant, earthy space.

Chasing the Cloud

A puppy jumps, trying to fetch,
A fluffy wisp, oh what a stretch!
It wears a bowtie, a sight so grand,
With friends who are rolling in the sand.

A child twirls in a silly hat,
While wind teases with a feathered spat.
Kites swoop down for a playful embrace,
Inviting the sun to join in the race.

Dogs bark loudly all around,
As laughter echoes from the ground.
Chasing shadows, they skip and bound,
A collection of smiles, joy unbound.

Amidst the giggles, clouds play coy,
In this patchwork sky, all filled with joy.
The puppy pounces, oh what a laugh,
In this world where dreams draw a craft.

Pinnacles of Passion

On rooftops high, a parade of flair,
Cats strutting in coats, they simply dare.
With neckties on, they aim for the sky,
In a rooftop shindig, oh my, oh my!

Frogs in tuxedos croak out a tune,
While bats hang upside down near the moon.
Chameleons change into polka dots,
Jiving along in their fanciful plots.

Birds clock in with tiny briefcases,
While raccoons laugh at the silly faces.
They juggle grapes, a fine roguish skill,
In a world where laughter gives a thrill.

With each outrageous outfit displayed,
They're living high in their comedy parade.
As the sun sets low, the fun still grows,
In this whimsical realm, where anything goes!

The Fringe of Wonder

In a garden of quirks, the plants all sway,
With tulips wearing hats on a whim today.
Daisies laugh with their petals all bright,
While butterflies shimmy under moonlight.

A hedgehog dons glasses, a scholar so wise,
Surveying the laughter beneath the skies.
Ladybugs dance, with tiny top hats,
Hosting a gala with all of their chats.

The moon winks down at the flowered spree,
As seedlings gossip about bumblebee.
In this corner, delight gives charade,
Each bloom a character that never will fade.

With laughter echoing from opening buds,
This whimsical realm, mired in floods,
Of joy and nonsense, each creature a part,
In the fringe of wonder, a comedic art.

The Summit's Embrace

Atop the hill, a cap so bright,
It flutters high, a comical sight.
A cozy crown, with style to spare,
It blows with the wind, the ultimate flair.

The breeze whispers tales of distant towns,
And giggles as it tumbles down.
With every tip, and playful toss,
That cap's no loss—just gain, not a dross.

Climbing peaks, we wear our cheer,
Every summit brings more hats near.
Rolling down, we chase with glee,
Who knew a cap would set us free?

So here we'll stand, 'neath skies so blue,
With laughter loud, and visions new.
Each stitch and seam, a merry trace,
In every hat, we find our place.

Peaks of Thought

Through lofty realms of fluffy dreams,
We toss our hats and hear the screams.
Eureka moments fly us high,
As brainwaves dance and levitate the sky.

Caps of color, spiked with charms,
Lead the way through thoughts that warm.
With every lift, ideas bloom,
In silly styles that banish gloom.

A monocle perched upon a head,
Gives strength to ponder what's ahead.
Laughter echoes in that misty air,
For those who dare to dream and dare!

So scale those heights, with wits and glee,
Like clowns on clouds, we're truly free.
In hats adorned with tales unfurled,
We tip our caps to this wild world.

Toppers and Treasures

Oh look at me, a king in cap,
With treasures rare, I'm taking a nap!
A hat of feathers, a plume so grand,
Each dream I clasp, with a lazy hand.

In jest, we find the funniest sights,
As toppers tumble in whimsical flights.
Gold coins shine 'neath the brim, you see,
Every chuckle unlocks a spree.

A jester's grin, I wear with ease,
Each quip a treasure, a merry tease.
Juggling hats, I toss with flair,
Gems of laughter fill the air.

So come and dance, join in the fun,
In this mad hatter's world, we've won.
For every joke that we create,
Is just a treasure that can't wait.

Celestial Canopies

Look at the sky, a canvas vast,
With dotted hats that are unsurpassed.
Each star dares wear a twinkling light,
As cosmic toppers, they shine so bright.

We gather under this cap so wide,
With laughter bubbling, let's not hide.
Galaxies spin in a fanciful dance,
Tickled by space, we take a chance.

Comets stream like hats on fire,
As planets wobble with fun conspire.
In this celestial dome, we play,
Crafting dreams as night meets day.

So let's tip our caps to the evening's cheer,
With giggles and stars, let's persevere.
In this tapestry of cosmic delight,
Every funny moment feels just right.

Fabrics of the Air

Fluffy clouds parade, a silly sight,
With birdies in bonnets taking flight.
A seagull's cap, a squirrel's toupee,
Who knew sky fashion could be so cliché?

Kites are the models, strings are the seams,
Dancing above like whimsical dreams.
A picnic blanket flutters, a rogue hat thief,
Wind steals the show, causing much grief.

Twirling umbrellas, umbrellas that laugh,
Chasing balloons in their playful path.
A parade of colors, a carnival spree,
Fabrics aloft in a fabric-y glee.

As laughter echoes, a farce in the breeze,
Birds strut their plumage with effortless ease.
The sky's their runway, a limitless flair,
In this fashion show high, nothing to wear!

Adorning Ambitions

A top hat on a turtle, oh what a sight,
With dreams of becoming a chef tonight.
His ladle held high, and a grin to the skies,
Who knew he could bake? What a clever surprise!

A llama in layers, all stylish and bold,
Glittery goggles that sparkle like gold.
She struts through the park, a diva supreme,
Dreaming of runways and winning the theme.

Funky fedoras planted on daisies,
They sway to the rhythm, feeling all hazy.
A snail in a sombrero, shaking its shell,
In the dance of ambition, all's merry and swell.

Blustery winds whip the silliness by,
As fluttering fabrics twist, turn and fly.
In the circus of dreams, with humor we share,
Adorning ambitions beyond compare!

Silhouettes on the Horizon

A shadowy figure with a floppy wide brim,
Dances on the edge where the sun starts to dim.
What lies beneath? A cat with a grin,
Who simply adores doing backflips in sin!

A barrel of laughter trails far in the sky,
With near-sighted owls who squint and ask why.
Their monocles glimmer, a theatrical play,
As they miss the horizon, then fly far away.

Balloons all giggle, wiggling their tails,
Casting odd shapes like mythical whales.
In the dusk's embrace, their colors collide,
Sailing through dreams, on the clouds they abide.

Under the glow of a twilight grand show,
Silhouettes prance with a whimsical flow.
In this playful ballet of dusk and delight,
Silliness reigns in the fading sunlight!

The Enigma of Elevation

Up in the air, a riddle unfolds,
Why are geese sporting hats made of gold?
With ties that are bright, and feathers so chic,
They gossip of clouds, styling all week.

A million balloons float up for the fun,
Each one a secret, not meant for the sun.
In a wink and a smile, they wiggle and sway,
Leaving giggles below as they drift far away.

A jester in flight, on a breeze he relies,
With a cap full of jokes, see the surprise!
As he flips through the atmosphere, cracking a pun,
Higher and higher, until he's outdone.

In this quandary of laughter, a twist of the tail,
A canopy of whimsy, a carnival sail.
Elevating the fun, from heights we adore,
With enigmas of joy, let's always explore!

Ceremonies of the Sky

A chapeau spins in the wind,
Like a dancer with a grin.
It twirls and dips with glee,
Painting dreams for all to see.

The bowler bounces up high,
Tipping low, oh my, oh my!
In the crowd, it steals the show,
With a flair that's quite the pro.

A top hat struts with pride,
While the beanie takes a ride.
Each one struts its quirky flair,
Leaving giggles in the air.

A sombrero on a kite,
Is a laugh that feels just right.
As they soar and float about,
Who wouldn't smile, twist, and shout?

Adornments in the Altitude

On an eagle's head a crown,
Wobbling high above the town.
Feathers, beads, and shiny bits,
A regal look that never quits.

A baseball cap takes a leap,
While a beret snuggles deep.
Each hat shares its wildest tales,
Like balloonists on the gales.

A beehive perched so spry,
Buzzing laughs as it flies by.
With every twist and every turn,
New antics for us all to learn.

A wizard's pointy hat spins fast,
Crafting spells with every blast.
As clouds chuckle and roll around,
In this circus, joy is found.

Eclipse of the Headpiece

A cap went wandering one day,
To catch the sun's golden ray.
It slipped from view, oh what a sight,
Dancing shadows, dark delight.

A beanie caught in a breeze,
Landed high among the trees.
Whispers echoed, "What a show!"
As squirrels clapped and started to go.

Fedoras flipping in the sky,
Sneaking peeks as they float by.
Each one waiting for its chance,
To land this kaleidoscope dance.

A redneck hat holds a beer,
While a fedora cheers and jeers.
With laughter lighting up the gloom,
They all wiggle for more room.

Stylish Journeys Beyond

A straw hat took a grand tour,
Leading dreams with panache, for sure.
Gliding over fields so green,
Bedecked with flowers, a charming scene.

A cap with ears jumped on a bike,
Wheeling fast, oh what a spike!
Chasing puddles, splashing with flair,
Who knew roads could hold such dare?

Toppling hats on a big parade,
Each one dancing, unafraid.
With every tip, a laughter burst,
In this chaos, joy was first.

A beaker on a rocket's head,
Flying high where few have tread.
With colors swirling, bold and bright,
In fun's embrace, they took to flight.

Chapeaus and Skylines

On rooftops, the funny capers soar,
A feathered friend opens quite the door.
Top hats dance with glee at the breeze,
While bowler hats giggle among the leaves.

The sun peeks out, tipping its own hat,
As wise old sombreros go splat!
They tumble and twirl, what a sight to see,
Juggling clouds, oh so carefree!

Pork pies wobble like jelly on high,
While bonnets flirt with the passing sky.
In this cap-lined world, laughter takes flight,
As silly headwear embraces delight.

So raise your chapeaus to the laughable scene,
Where whimsy and wonder are truly serene.
For every skyline tells a funny tale,
With each playful headpiece, let joy prevail.

A Crown of Dreams

In the town where jesters wear their crowns,
The dreamers spin, never feeling down.
With silly sequins and glittering threads,
Their laughter flows where the silly strolls tread.

A sky full of dreams, a floating parade,
Where whimsies are made, and antics displayed.
With jester's caps tipped just a bit too far,
They laugh at the clouds, wishing on a star.

Chasing rainbows like butterflies bright,
In this kingdom of giggles, all feels just right.
With each twist of the breeze, a new joke unravels,
As dreams take wing on whimsical travels.

So wear your crown and dance through the day,
For with laughter around, who needs the gray?
In this patchwork of joy, we find true bliss,
A funny crown where we all can reminisce.

The Brim's Gaze

With brims that peek over the edge of the sky,
I spy a curious cloud flutter by.
A straw hat chuckles, casting its shade,
While sunflowers grin at the games we've played.

Top hats tip down, grinning wide with delight,
Casting shadows that dance in the light.
While floppy hats wiggle, jiving around,
In a world full of whimsy, pure joy's found.

The sunny sky blushes, wearing a smile,
As the charm of these headpieces goes on for a while.
With each lazy gust, hear them giggle away,
In a raucous embrace of a fun-filled day.

So let the brims whisper, let the stories soar,
In the thrumming heartbeat of laughter's core.
For in this funny land where the spirits roam,
Each cap tells a tale, each cloud is our home.

Relics of the Skyline

Among the tall towers, past laughter and light,
Old relics of laughter take joyous flight.
With tattered old fedoras spinning around,
Making mischief while winking at the ground.

A tiara twirls like a top on a spree,
As chivalrous beanies bring toast to the tea.
These treasures of joy soar high in the air,
Mirth nestled gently in every wear.

Floppy felt hats wear a feathered grin,
As umbrella hats plot where trouble begins.
Each flap and each tilt gives a nod to the day,
Where dreams take flight, and we giggle away.

So gather 'round relics of joy and cheer,
Let laughter outshine every doubt and fear.
With each skyline story, let the fun unfold,
In this whimsical dance where joy can be told.

Dreamscapes Awaits

In a land where toppers play,
They dance and twirl in bright array,
A somersault, a cartwheel round,
With flying chapeaus they astound.

A beanie tossed, a fedora flies,
The giggles echo, reach the skies,
A bucket leaps, a crown takes flight,
Laughter reigns from morn till night.

A zany parade beneath the sun,
Each headpiece claiming it's the one,
While socks on hands are trying to wave,
The funniest fashion, none can save.

When dreams take shape atop our heads,
And silliness is what it spreads,
In a world of whim, let's celebrate,
The joy that's found, it's never late!

Horizons in Retreat

The sun dips low, the sky's a mess,
An octopus dons a sailor's dress,
With kraken hats doing a jig,
Each creature winks, it's all so big.

A llama prances, wearing shades,
With rainbow socks that never fade,
A cheerio bows with sugar sprinkles,
While jellybeans bounce, and laughter twinkles.

The clouds all giggle, plump and white,
As squirrels in berets take to flight,
They cartwheel through the breezy day,
Playing tag in a silly way.

When evening falls, the stars appear,
A chandelier hangs, oh so near,
With each odd hat that cracks a smile,
The retreating day brightens a while!

The Above and the Adorned

In the realm of whimsical trends,
An elephant wears, what fun transcends,
A top hat perched upon its trunk,
With drumsticks marching, oh so punk!

A poodle sports a pirate cap,
And dances round, a jolly slap,
With rubber chickens by its side,
They pirouette, in joy and pride.

In the skies, balloons join in,
Twirling hats made of lost tin,
Each one dreaming of a flight,
While goofy giggles fill the night.

With every plume and every lace,
Confetti heads, all share the space,
In this grand carnival of cheer,
The above and adorned draw us near!

A Tapestry of Transit

On trains where slippers steal the show,
A conductor wears a hat of dough,
With cinnamon swirls upon his head,
Together we ride, where dreams are spread.

A bicycle zips with wobbly grace,
A panda bobs in a crazy race,
With sippy cups and biscuits crisp,
All aboard for a joyous lisp.

A wagon rolls with hats of cheese,
As cats wear crowns with utmost ease,
The scenery shifts, a silly spree,
Transforming all who come to see.

In transit's realm of giggly fun,
Where every journey weighs a ton,
A tapestry woven with playful cheer,
Binds every heart as they draw near!

Threads of Tomorrow

With colors bright and patterns wild,
A playful cap upon a child.
They tip their head to catch a breeze,
And dance about with joyous ease.

Each thread a tale, each stitch a laugh,
As they parade their goofy craft.
In every twist, a secret lies,
A world of fun beneath those skies.

The future's shaped in yarn and cheer,
With silly shapes we hold so dear.
A beanie here, a feather there,
Tomorrow's whims float through the air.

So gather 'round, it's time to play,
With silly styles that lead the way.
In every curl and twist we find,
A treasure chest of joy combined.

Ascending Attire

Up, up, up the tops we climb,
In jaunty caps that chime with rhyme.
A bowler bounces, a beret twirls,
Through swirling winds, our laughter swirls.

A feathered friend upon my head,
Takes my worries, makes them shed.
I tip it with a playful wink,
And ponder where the clouds may sink.

With every step, our spirits rise,
In silly hats that touch the skies.
We chase the sun with giddy glee,
In outfits bold, we roam so free.

The journey's bright, the vibe is right,
As hats take flight, what a sight!
With twists and turns, we strut around,
With giggles mixed in every sound.

Canvas Crowns and Clouded Seasons

A cap made of canvas, oh what a sight,
It floats like a cloud, so fluffy and light.
When rainy days loom over head,
This crown of fun keeps worries fed.

In seasons changing, colors collide,
A canvas smile we simply can't hide.
Each splash of paint a chuckle ignites,
A masterpiece of silly delights.

We chase the puffs, the suns, the rains,
With whimsical wear, we break all chains.
Dancing through puddles, splashing with glee,
In our vibrant canvas, we're wild and free!

So let's make memories, let's paint the air,
With laughter and joy, we have enough to share.
In every season, let's wear our dreams,
And float through life on laughter's beams.

Pointed Peaks and Dapper Dreams

In pointed peaks that reach for the stars,
Dapper dreams glide on fashion's cars.
With laughter loud, we tip our tips,
As we sashay with enthusiastic skips.

Oh, dapper fellows with silken bows,
With every dash our charm just grows.
A pointed hat from yesteryear,
Makes us giggle and brings us cheer.

We gather round in mismatched styles,
And share our tales that stretch for miles.
With dreams so bright, and spirits high,
We twirl with joy beneath the sky.

So let's ascend to peaks of fun,
In dapper threads, we're never done!
With every twist, there's magic, it seems,
Pointed peaks fuel our wild dreams.

Daring Heights

A top hat danced upon a breeze,
It took a leap with such great ease.
A bowler rolled and spun around,
While a sunhat laughed without a sound.

On rooftops high, they played a game,
Of hopscotch skies and hat-flung fame.
With each big jump, a silly shout,
Those hats were what it's all about!

A beret twirled, a sombrero spun,
They giggled loud, oh what a fun!
With every fall, a silly flip,
These daring caps could never trip.

So up they soared, the view divine,
As hats flew high, each one a sign.
Of laughter, joy, and pure delight,
In playful heights, they took their flight.

Beyond the Limitless

A wacky cap with polka dots,
Said, 'Let's climb the chili pots!'
A beanie grinned with extra flair,
And promised fun was waiting there.

Through the clouds, they made a dash,
Each cap hoping for a splash.
With every leap, a giggle burst,
Age of worry? Never first!

A fedora twitched and took a bow,
Demanding fun without a cow.
While sunflowers peeked up to see,
What wild tricks the hats could be!

They glided down from peaks so grand,
With hair-flings fast and hats unplanned.
What joy, what cheer, what endless play,
Those friendly caps shone bright all day.

The Echo of Elevation

Up in the clouds, a beret yelled,
'Come join the fun, let's not be held!'
A straw hat floated, light as air,
Echoing laughter everywhere.

With every bounce, they sang a note,
As wind carried each playful quote.
A chapeau tipped its brim so wide,
And twirled around with silly pride.

Through breezy gates, they chased the sound,
Where every giggle knew no ground.
An umbrella twirled, brought rainy dates,
In leaps of joy, they danced like mates.

Above the world, they sang their tune,
Under the bright and giggly moon.
These caps in flight, a sight to see,
Echoing laughter, wild and free.

Caps and Beyond

A cap with flair and colors bright,
Dreamed of dancing through the night.
It twirled, it spun, it hopped so high,
While birds above just laughed and sighed.

The caps convened in a fun brigade,
Mapping pathways where giggles played.
With each wild leap, they formed a chain,
As all around, they spread the gain.

A beanie tossed a pie in jest,
While others plotted their next quest.
Through giggly trails, they slipped and rolled,
A tale of fun, forever told.

No limits found, just silly glee,
For every cap dreamed wildly free.
With laughter loud and spirits high,
They painted joy across the sky.

Plumage of the Sky

Colorful crowns go floating by,
On heads in clouds, oh my, oh my!
A bird in a bowler, quite the sight,
Winks at a pigeon, taking flight.

A tinfoil crown on a dog so proud,
Struts like a king, head in the clouds.
Silly sombreros on squirrels who prance,
Dancing around, giving nature a chance.

With paper cranes perched on the breeze,
A jester's cap hangs from tall trees.
Bubblegum hats that spin and pop,
Roll down the hill, laugh 'til we drop!

Plumage of colors that tickle the air,
Each silly hat brings a smile to share.
Under the sun, in a jubilant sway,
Who knew the sky had so much to play?

Clouds Above

Fluffy shapes with a whimsical twist,
A pancake cat that we can't resist.
Top hats tumble and gumdrops soar,
Chasing down rainbows that beg us for more.

The sneaky sun peeks through a veil,
Tickling feathers on a fluffy whale.
With marshmallow dreams softly spread,
Adventurous visions dance in our heads.

Caps of cheese and hats of pie,
Frolic in fields where giggles fly high.
A parade of pigeons in vibrant attire,
Flutter and flap, never seem to tire!

Silly clouds with their playful jest,
Making us giggle, this is the best!
Catch a cap as it flutters past,
A day full of laughter, made to last!

Caps Below

In a tiny town with a quirky view,
Every head dons a hat, that's true!
Cabbage caps and pirate's glee,
Swirling in dizzying jubilee.

A cat with a sombrero sips his tea,
While mice in tiaras dance with glee.
Jellybean top hats wobble ahead,
On tiny heads, like stories spread.

Giraffes in beanies peek over the fence,
Their whimsical ways, making no sense.
Each charming cap tells tales so wild,
Lively and laughable, just like a child.

In this town where fun takes charge,
Laughter erupts, and joys enlarge.
Beneath the wide sky, all hats in tow,
A jubilant sea of caps on show!

Adornments of Ambition

A wizard's hat made of whipped cream,
Glides through the air like a playful dream.
Chasing a dragon with pockets of loam,
Each whimsical hat leads us to roam.

In pursuit of wishes, we gather round,
A fortress of hats, laughter unbound.
Tentacled toppers of daring flair,
Whirl into wonder, we've not a care.

A rubber duck crowned with blissful pride,
Waddles through puddles on a joyful ride.
Each new adornment a giggle in bloom,
As we dance with delight in an airborne room!

Ambition beams through each feathered style,
With laughter as fuel, we journey a mile.
In this crown of giggles, we sail through the sky,
Dreams twirling higher as we laugh and fly!

The Lofty Pursuit

A quest for style, oh what a delight,
As we chase our hats into the night.
Galactic helmets and crowns made of jelly,
Dancing with stars that tickle the belly.

Chasing a breeze that's full of surprise,
Balloons and bonnets float through the skies.
A picnic of laughter, each gem a delight,
As kooky as biscuits in moonlight.

In corners of wonder, we glance and we grin,
A tapestry woven with fluffy whimsy thin.
With helmets of cheese and hats of gold,
Each one a story waiting to be told.

So let's lift our crowns and let laughter flow,
In this lofty pursuit, we'll put on a show!
With each joyful minute, we'll leap and we'll twirl,
For the fun never ends in this rhyming world!

The View from Up High

With a feathered crown on my head,
I thought I'd take a look instead.
From my perch upon a stack of books,
I saw the world with funny looks.

The clouds waved back, a fluffy jest,
As squirrels danced on their tiny quest.
I shouted down, 'Come join the ride!'
But they just rolled their eyes and sighed.

A pigeon flew by, took my hat,
Said, 'You're too silly for a chat!'
I laughed so hard, almost fell down,
'This view is best, oh, what a clown!'

So here I sit, a king of jest,
With laughter echoing from the west.
The world below, a stage so bright,
Where everyone's a little light.

Layers of Imagined Paths

In a tangle of colorful threads,
I wander paths where nonsense spreads.
A bearded goat in a beret,
Kept insisting we must play today!

A basket on my head, quite snazzy,
Each step I took got more and jazzy.
Winding trails with giggles and grins,
Upside-down thoughts, tumbling spins.

With every twist, I lost my shoe,
The goat just laughed, 'You should wear two!'
But who needs footwear when you can prance?
In pants made of candy, take a chance!

So we danced through the mishmash of fun,
Chasing giggles as bright as the sun.
Every layer peeled back revealed,
The joy of silliness, forever sealed.

In the Shade of Aspirations

Beneath a tree with a funny face,
I dreamt of journeys to outer space.
My dreams wore slippers and a cape,
Chasing stars at a lightning pace.

A snail slipped by, wearing a tie,
Said, 'Why not aim for the pie in the sky?'
I agreed, 'With sprinkles, I'll take a slice!'
Then we giggled at the thought of that price.

A wobbly sunbeam sent us a wink,
'Chase your dreams, but stop for a drink!'
The tree chuckled and shook its leaves,
As we pondered all the jokes life weaves.

In that shade, we planned and played,
A realm of laughter our minds portrayed.
With each giggle, our spirits soared,
In a world where silliness is adored.

The Crest of Curiosity

On the crest of a hill, my thoughts took flight,
With a hat made of clouds, oh what a sight!
A curious cat with glasses so round,
Said, 'Come, let's explore the upside-down ground.'

We found a bench made of jellybeans,
Sat sipping sunshine like two silly queens.
With each bounce, our laughter rang clear,
Turning the mundane into pure cheer.

Around us swirled a confetti breeze,
Whispers of whimsy in the rustling trees.
'What's next?' asked the cat, eyes all aglow,
I replied, 'Let's see where the laughter will go!'

So here we remain, with stardust and glee,
Creating tales only friends can see.
At the crest of curiosity, we reside,
Where nonsense blooms, and joy can't hide.

Veils of Vision

In the bustling bazaar, a funny sight,
A giant sombrero, oh what a fright!
People chuckle and point, a sight so rare,
Who knew headgear could cause such a scare?

Next comes a beret, perched with flair,
It wobbles and jostles, does it even care?
With every step taken, it jigs and sways,
A dance of the wild, in whimsical ways.

The top hats are tipping, the bowlers will bow,
A parade of silliness, oh look at that cow!
It dons a fedora, all leather and gleam,
In a world full of laughter, a true hat dream.

So when you see headwear, remember to grin,
For each quirky cover helps the fun begin!
In the land of the odd, where the wild styles roam,
Every silly topper feels just like home.

Toppers Under Twilight

Under the moonlight, with styles so bold,
A fish in a helmet, oh what a hold!
It zooms through the air, a glimmering spree,
As laughter erupts from a lemon tree.

A cap with a propeller spins head over heels,
While a pirate's bandana reveals all his feels.
With each twist and turn, under starlit skies,
Night brings out giggles, oh how time flies!

A baker with a toque, the flour goes high,
Sprinkling the world like a pie in the sky.
And a sombrero tilted, with a cheeky charm,
Keeps everyone laughing with its vibrant calm.

So if you should wander, and hats catch your eye,
Join in the fun, give the lighthearted a try!
With laughter as our guide, and joy as our aim,
The night will remember our wonderful game.

The Canvas of the Cosmos

In a world painted bright where the colors collide,
A helmet with feathers takes quite a ride.
It swoops by the stars, a whimsical twist,
Creating a cosmos that can't be missed.

Next, there's a cowboy, with boots made of glue,
His ten-gallon hat tells stories anew.
It wobbles and bounces, as he dances a jig,
In the hall of the funny, that's how he digs!

A crown made of cheese and a scarf of the moon,
The ensembles get wilder, they start quite a tune.
Laughing and spinning, we join in the craze,
Where fashion is silly, and time slips away.

So gaze at the skies, where the oddballs play,
In this gallery of laughter, we won't shy away!
With a twirl and a giggle, life's a grand art,
Each head-spinning moment, a joy to impart.

Shadows of Silk

In the corners of dusk, where the sillies abide,
A hat made of shadows begins to slide.
With fanciful shapes that wiggle and sway,
They tease and they tickle, in a playful display.

A bowler that jingles with laughter and cheer,
Whispers to passersby, 'Come dance over here!'
And a floppy sun hat, in stripes oh so bright,
Twirls in a whirl, like a firefly's light.

A pirate's eye patch, adorned with a grin,
Winks at the universe, let the fun begin!
With swirls made of silk dancing freely around,
The shadows do stories, where joy can be found.

So let's raise our voices, let's raise up our hats,
To the tales that we weave, with jesters and bats.
In the twilight's embrace, let our laughter take flight,
For in this silk dreamland, we'll dance through the night.

The Elevation of Dreams

A chapeau flew upon the breeze,
It danced and twirled with such great ease.
A rabbit wore it with grand style,
And hopped along, all cheeky smile.

A turtle tried, it spun around,
But on its back, it hit the ground.
The hat declared, "I'm not a toy!"
While squirrels laughed, oh what a joy!

Up high it soared and just looked down,
At all the creatures of the town.
With every gust, it took a chance,
To lead the critters in a dance!

Yet in the end, it met a tree,
And what a flap, oh dearie me!
It lost its flair, but not its cheer,
For every laugh might draw it near.

Tipping the Scale of Day

A jaunty cap sat on a cat,
It claimed it could predict a spat.
With every swish, it'd tilt and twirl,
While chasing mice with a little whirl.

At noon it jumped onto the shed,
With dreams of cheese, it dashed ahead.
But hats behave in fickle ways,
And ended up lost in a bag of hay.

An ant came by, bit firmly down,
On what it thought was quite a crown.
"This isn't food!" the hat complained,
While trying to dodge the little bane.

The day was saved by a flock of birds,
Who flew in squawking with funny words.
They rescued it before night fell,
And wore it proudly, all was well!

A Canvas Above

A floppy lid on a painter's head,
With colors splashed, it was joy instead.
It bobbed about like a floaty boat,
While birds admired and joined the note.

Each stroke that flew across the sky,
Was polka-dotted, oh my my!
The palette spilled with every turn,
As clouds below began to churn.

A gust of wind brought laughter loud,
As patches flapped, a vibrant crowd.
The sun just chuckled at the view,
Saying, "Now, that's a clever crew!"

When night fell down, the hues were lost,
The hat had fun but paid the cost.
It snuggled close in a comfy nook,
A canvas dreaming with every look.

Chasing the Sun's Glow

A busy beanie on a bee,
Buzzing around, so wild and free.
It danced on flowers and took a dive,
In search of rays to come alive.

A kite spun high, forgets its string,
In playful jumps, it starts to swing.
It spun along with joy so bright,
While catching glimmers of warm sunlight.

A whimsy hat fell near a brook,
And into antics, it gladly took.
It wobbled on rocks with every hop,
While giggling bubbles went "pop pop pop!"

As shadows stretched and day grew dim,
The hat then laughed and gave a whim.
Chasing warmth till the stars would show,
With silly tales of high and low.

Whenever the Wind Whispers

The breeze picked my cap, took it for a run,
It twirled and it twisted, oh what a fun!
Chasing it down was quite the grand show,
I laughed as I stumbled, tripped over my toe.

A beret on a dog, looking quite chic,
He strutted around, oh so unique!
With every sharp turn, I burst out in glee,
That pup in a toque, a sight to see.

A sombrero flew past, took a dive in the lake,
The ducks thought it food, for goodness' sake!
Waltzing with waves, it floated away,
Laughter erupted, brightening the day.

As wind swirls around, causing all this mess,
I'm left with my scarf, oh what a dress!
But each twist and turn brings a smile so bright,
Windy adventures, pure comedic delight.

Shadows Under Canopies

Beneath leafy branches, a festival spry,
A sunhat misheard the chatter nearby.
It danced with the breeze, shook feathers with flair,
As sunglasses giggled, waving without care.

A top hat with winks, boasting tales so grand,
Broke into a jig—oh, wasn't it planned?
With a tap and a twirl, it stole all the cheer,
While everyone wondered, "Is it really here?"

The sun took a break, slipped under the trees,
Yet all hats conspired to flow with the breeze.
In shadows they swayed, threw a party so loud,
Each brimful of laughter—a jubilant crowd.

At dusk, as we gathered, my beanie stole sight,
With a magical glow, it gleamed in the night.
While shadows were dancing and giggles took flight,
It's hats that unite us, what a comical sight!

The Journey of Headgear

A beanie once dreamed of the high snowy peaks,
But ended up hanging with other lost freaks.
They plotted and schemed, for adventures so free,
A fashion parade, oh where would it be?

A fedora flipped over, "To the shore!" it called,
While earmuffs just sighed, "Let's not get too balled."
When bonnets invented a game of their own,
They played hide and seek, in wild turf overgrown.

A crown soon arrived, oh so regal and bold,
With jewels that shimmered, and stories retold.
Yet every great party needs laughter in tow,
So they traded their crowns for a wild limbo show!

In the end they agreed, life's a colorful spree,
With caps that can chatter and families so free.
Thanks to the voyage, the friendships so dear,
They tossed all their worries, and cheered loud with cheer!

Orbiting the Unknown

A space cap took flight, with stars around it,
Zooming through cosmos, like a playful skit.
Asteroids chuckled as they wheeled and spun,
To think that a cap could have so much fun!

With a visor that glimmered like a shot from the sun,
It dodged comets and laughed while it spun.
Yet every new planet that came into view,
Had hats of its own, all out to pursue.

A helmet from Mars tried to dance with a twirl,
While sombreros from Neptune began to unfurl.
They exchanged goofy looks, shared jokes from afar,
And claimed every moon with their hysterical star.

Orbiting wildly, now who's having fun?
They giggled and clattered; the adventure's begun.
For in every odd corner of this cosmic play,
It's hats causing laughter, all night and all day!

Dreams Beyond the Dome

I wore a cap made of cheese,
It smelled like my favorite breeze.
My dreams took flight on a whim,
Chasing clouds, oh so slim.

A beret danced with pure delight,
Twirl it under the moonlight.
With every flip, a giggle soared,
As fashion became my playful sword.

A sombrero caught the sun's bright gaze,
Reflecting light in funky ways.
I laughed as it spun and twirled,
In a world where joy unfurled.

Riding rainbows in a top hat grand,
With pockets full of grains of sand.
Adventures fit for every head,
In the land where silliness is bred.

The Fashioned Frontier

At the edge of style, I did stand,
In a bowler, looking quite grand.
With polka dots and stripes so bold,
The stories of the west were old.

A ten-gallon hat on a tiny head,
I leaped and laughed, no place for dread.
Fashioned dreams danced in the sky,
With every twirl, I felt so spry.

A coral fedora caught the breeze,
I chased it down with matching knees.
In a world where nonsense reigns,
With laughter spilling like wild rains.

Cowboy boots with glittery toes,
Where silly fashion freely flows.
Shimmering in the sunset glow,
As freedom's laughter starts to grow.

A Voyage in Fabric

A pirate cap with a feather bright,
Set sail on waves of pure delight.
Swabbing decks with a wink of mischief,
In a world where fashion's no stiff.

In jackets made of softest dreams,
I floated high on silken beams.
My shoes were made of jelly beans,
And laughter burst at every seam.

A scarf that danced in the gentle air,
Wrapped around stories, rich and rare.
With colors bright, it leaped and twirled,
In this fabric, joy unfurled.

Upon a boat of velvet shades,
Waves of laughter threw parades.
A fabric world, so full of fun,
A voyage where we all outrun.

The Echoes of Elevation

In a top hat perched on a mountain high,
I waved to clouds that drifted by.
With echoes ringing in my ear,
I danced with shadows, faced my fear.

A beanie sported with a grin,
Launched me higher, oh what a spin!
Each twist and leap, a laugh or two,
In a realm where silly dreams came true.

Gliding on a carpet made of plaid,
I called it 'home,' it drove me mad.
With every bump, I laughed aloud,
Floating higher above the crowd.

Atop the heights, where giggles reign,
I waved at valleys, felt no pain.
For in this joyous elevation,
Lies the fun of wild creation.

Skyline Silhouettes

Up high they sway, the toppers bold,
Funny shapes in the sunlight gold.
Each one a tale, a grand design,
Making cities laugh, oh how they shine!

A feathered friend on a rooftop peak,
Waves at the clouds, without a squeak.
The skyline grins with quirky flair,
As silly hats dance in the air.

A top hat hops, a beret rolls,
Playing tag with distant shoals.
Misfits unite in patterns bright,
Creating chaos, bringing delight!

So when you gaze at the view so wide,
Look closely for the laughter inside.
For every cap tells a joke or two,
Underneath the sky so blue!

Fabric and Flight

Stitched with secrets, they catch the breeze,
Whirling and twirling like dandelion seeds.
Each fabric snap makes a giggling sound,
As whimsy takes flight, joy unbound!

A polka dot scarf sails on by,
Waving hello to the passing sky.
Patchwork panels dance in a rush,
Chasing the clouds in a jolly hush!

In cherry red, or blue so bright,
Cloth creatures fall with all their might.
Laughter erupts as they tumble down,
In a carnival caper, no time to frown!

So, let's gather our bolts and thread,
Vista of laughter, where we tread.
For every stitch has a smile to share,
In a world where fabric rules the air!

The Edge of Elegance

Upon the precipice, they take their place,
Wacky crowns with a formal grace.
Tiaras teeter, and bowler hats spin,
As fashion's whimsy invites a grin.

Pearls and polka dots blend with flair,
Dapper shades flash with a daring air.
A monocle winks with a cheeky tease,
Challenging norms, oh, what a breeze!

In this gala of giggles, style feels loose,
A tuxedo cat sips a juice.
Toppling over, they all conspire,
To balance on edges that never tire!

So grab your bow ties and quirky ties tight,
At the edge of elegance, we revel in light.
With each wobble, we cheer and shout,
For nonsense and style are what it's about!

Twilight Toppers

As sunsets roll over the sleepy town,
Mismatched headwear starts to clown.
A wizard's hat meets a sunhat grand,
In a twilight dance, oh, isn't it planned?

Glow-in-the-dark and sequins too,
They tilt and tilt in a starry view.
Surreal tidings wrap round the head,
As giggles echo, dreams are spread!

A cap and gown, a pirate's quest,
They spark joy from the very best.
Under fading skies, they banter and tease,
Among swirls of laughter, they glide with ease!

So as night settles, and the stars leap,
Hats share secrets, and they don't keep.
For in twilight's gleam, they frolic and play,
Chasing the laughter till break of day!

Crowns of Adventurers

Upon our heads, we wear our crowns,
Crafted from laughter, joy, and frowns.
With every tip and playful bow,
We reign as jesters, take a vow.

Explorers bold in search of cheer,
Our merry gathering draws them near.
With wibbly-wobbly, twisty flair,
We dance like monkeys, without a care.

Papers flutter, feathers fly,
In our whimsical parade, oh my!
We've mixed the funky with the fun,
While chaos sparkles in the sun.

Each crown a story woven tight,
Of daring dreams and silly sights.
We'll wear them proudly, laughter loud,
In this wild and noble, jester crowd.

The Skyward Gaze

Upward we look, with hats askew,
Chasing clouds that pretend to moo.
With misplaced visions and whimsical fears,
We giggle at stars, and toast our beers.

Wishing on wishes that might just flop,
As pigeons fly by, we hug the top.
Each glance a treasure, with tales untold,
Whirling in laughter, being bold.

When the sun winks, and moonlight stares,
Our heads collide with the light, without cares.
Fanciful dreams fly high and wide,
In this enchanting, silly ride.

Skyward we leap, embracing our fate,
With playful hats, we celebrate!
Let's joke with the breezes and sway with the trees,
In the laughter-filled air, as we do as we please.

Whispers of the Wide Open

In the open fields, the whispers call,
With tunes so silly, we dance and sprawl.
Hats made of daisies, wild and bright,
They giggle along from morning to night.

Every breeze brings a chuckle or two,
As butterflies flit in a grand debut.
With each fluttering friend that joins the parade,
We share our secrets, unafraid.

Amidst the grass, we roll and play,
Wearing our hearts as ties of the day.
In this meadow, where giggles ignite,
Full of whimsy and endless delight.

So here's to the stories of fields so wide,
Where hats bloom freely, no place to hide.
With every twirl and every glance,
We sway to the rhythm of a silly dance.

Fabrics of Freedom

We stitch our dreams in vibrant thread,
With whims of zest, winks come instead.
Each fabric a tale, of wild delight,
In patterns of laughter, colors so bright.

Freedom wears a quirky grin,
In wobbly hats, it twirls and spins.
With each flutter, threads come alive,
In this tapestry, we thrive and jive.

Bold and unique, we choose our style,
As giggles weave along the mile.
We gather the colors from skies above,
In this wild sewing, we share our love.

So here's to the moments that make us sing,
In a whirl of fabric, joy takes wing.
With every seam and every swish,
We craft our freedom, our heart's own wish.

www.ingramcontent.com/pod-product-compliance
Lightning Source LLC
Chambersburg PA
CBHW070002300426
43661CB00141B/146